Walks wi

i

Yorkshire Dales

MALHAM &
AIREDALE

Mary Welsh

A QUESTA Guide

© Mary Welsh 2007

ISBN 978-1-898808-24-4

Published by
Questa Publishing Ltd., PO Box 520, Bamber Bridge,
Preston, Lancashire PR5 8LF
and printed by
Carnmor Print, 95/97 London Road, Preston,
Lancashire PR1 4BA

Contents

Introduction

Malham and Airedale

The limestone of the Craven Uplands, centred on Malham, is an almost horizontal high-level plateau. On its southern and western edges it is bounded by faults – uplifted strata of rock – which occurred millions of years ago. These faults are seen, for example, at Gordale Scar, Giggleswick Scar and Malham Cove. The line of the Mid-Craven fault traverses Kirkby Fell, Pikedaw and Gordale.

Malhamdale is a mere 8km (5 miles) long, and it is spectacular for all its length. The first walk in this book takes you along the side of Malham Tarn, a lime-rich upland lake. From it issues a small beck known as Malham Water, which once continued down the valley now aptly named Dry Valley and tumbled over Malham Cove in a spectacular waterfall.

After the last ice-age Malham Water disappeared at Water Sinks (a chaos of boulders) and Malham Cove waterfall ceased to exist. A stream does flow from an aperture at the foot of the Cove, but scientists using chemical tests found that this is not the overflow from the Tarn but comes from elsewhere on Malham Moor. The stream that disappears at Water Sinks emerges at Aire Head (below the village of Malham) as a trickle and adds its water to Malham Beck and Gordale Beck. The united waters become the River Aire and carry on eventually to become a mighty river.

Airedale, which merges into Malhamdale, has little of the drama of the upper dale. It is softer and wooded but, as with Malhamdale, high above the river lie great stretches of remote moorland, with small oases of fields surrounding sturdy farmhouses. It has tiny peaceful hamlets of fine houses and cottages. Kirkby Malham, with its majestic parish church, lies close to the River Aire and is the hub of this part of the dale. Too soon the river reaches Gargrave and swings away east, to become industrialised for much of its length.

This little book covers all of Malhamdale and also Airedale from its head to Gargrave. Parents embarking on these rambles might encourage the youngsters to notice the changing characteristics of the various areas. See if they can spot any differences in the habitats and if they can suggest a reason for this. Get them to spot the bird that is singing and then help them to identify it. Encourage them to begin to memorise the calls.

Persuade them to take over the map reading and perhaps teach them to use a compass to help with route finding. As the family progresses on the walks, discuss the weather and look for warning signs – cloud formations, hazy sunlight, changes in temperature and wind direction.

These walks are intended to introduce young people to hill-walking. They vary in length and are all on rights-of-way.

Above all, help the youngsters to enjoy the walks. Start with the shorter walks and work up to the more demanding ones. In such a way hill walking in such a glorious area will set youngsters off on what could become a compulsive, lifelong and extremely healthy pastime.

This is a great area to explore. However, the weather can change from blue sunny skies to rain clouds in a short time, so make sure all the family have some warm, waterproof clothing with them, even in the valleys. For these walks light-weight and well waterproofed boots are generally to be preferred. Families should carry what they expect to need in the way of food and water – stocking-up points can be few and far between.

During the walk it might be a good time to discuss with the youngsters the following points from

The Country Code
Enjoy the countryside and respect its life and work
Guard against all risk of fire
Fasten all gates
Keep to public paths across farmland
Use gates and stiles to cross fences, hedges and walls
Leave livestock, crops and machinery alone
Take your litter home. Help to keep all water clean
Protect wildlife, plants and trees
Take special care on country roads
Make no unnecessary noise.

1
Malham Tarn

*Malham Tarn is a lime-rich upland lake, set amid a variety of
habitats. It nestles at an altitude of 375m and is one of
Yorkshire's most attractive areas of open water, even in winter
time. From here the walk takes you on to limestone fell, followed
by some road walking along a narrow walled way. At Darnbrook it
descends a little to cross Cowside Beck and then comes a long
but steady climb over high limestone pastures to join the
Monk's Road (path), which continues all the way to the Tarn.*

Start: Water Sinks parking area (GR895657) on the north
side of the fell road and east of the gate.

Total distance: (11.3km) 7 miles

Height gain: 160m (525ft)

Difficulty: Moderate. Youngsters may find the climb from
Cowside Beck a little long.

1 From the back of the parking area, walk north along the
signposted Pennine Way, in the direction of magnificent
Highfolds Scar. Soon Malham Tarn comes into view and the
grassy trod brings you close beside it, where Malham Beck
issues from the lake. From here you can see a variety of duck
on the tranquil water, with Malham Tarn House on the opposite
bank, decked on either side by a boathouse. Follow the wide
green swathe as it bears steadily right across open pasture to
join, just before a gate, a reinforced track. Beyond, carry on
along the way, with Great Scar ahead. Notice how the young
trees have drystone walls around them and then compare
these trees with the mature trees, planted much earlier and
not walled. The trunks reveal the damage caused by grazing
animals.

2 Walk on beside the tarn and then cross the cattle grid into fine
deciduous woodland. Head on the way as it winds round the
gracious house, now Malham Tarn field centre. Continue on
away from the house, and look out for the steps, on the left,
to a little railed viewing platform. A short way, further on along
the track, a signposted path leads to a bird hide, from where
you can enjoy the myriad birds that live or feed on the water.
(Binoculars would make this more exciting.) Then as you near
the edge of the woodland, watch out for a signposted gate, on

Darnbrook House

Malham Tarn House

Malham Tarn

Middle House

Middle House Farm

START

the right, which you take to stroll on along the Pennine Way.

3 Walk the delightful grassy trod, which soon leads you out into a buttercup meadow and then between limestone hillocks. Go through the next gate and walk on with the wall to your left. Go past a single storey barn and where the track divides take either branch. Both run parallel with the wall, and soon join up and head on towards Great Hill farm, away to the left. Climb a ladder-stile and walk on over limestone upland to come to the corner where the wall turns left and there is a signpost for the Pennine Way, directing you left.

4 Descend to a signposted stile beside a locked gate. Bear right and then curve left over a hillock to follow a clear path that leads you on to join the narrow, walled fell road. Turn right and carry on, with care, as you could meet the occasional vehicle. Half way along there is a good grassy verge that makes for an easier walk. Then descend the steepish hill towards pretty Darnbrook Farm, snug in its hollow. Just before the house and on the right side of the road, go through a gate with a signpost post beside it, but at the time of writing, missing its direction arm.

5 Keep parallel with the wall on the right to climb a step-stile, marked by a yellow topped post. Go on to keep right of a bank barn and then head down to a ladder-stile. Beyond, cross a pool on flagstones and then a footbridge. Wind a little right and then curve round left to follow a path that climbs steadily.

When you reach a small shelf on the hillside, look right to see a blue ringed waymarker and turn right. Follow the path as it winds left and continues to climb the slope to a wall gap.

6 Carry on the fairly level way and then climb steadily to pass through a derelict wall. Stroll on through an area of limestone outcrops and go on to a locked gate. Climb the stile beside it and walk ahead on a clear path. As you wind round a limestone hillock a clump of trees comes into view. At the signpost you join Monk's Road, a path that has traversed the high slopes from Arncliffe. Turn right and walk the good track that continues on, passing behind a derelict farm almost lost in the trees spotted earlier. Continue ahead when the wall on your left turns down left, to walk on to come to a cross of tracks.

7 Walk left to another locked gate to climb the ladder-stile beside it. Descend a little and then take, on the right, a wide trod gently descending in a long curve (the Monk's Road) to climb a stile and then walk uphill, with the trees on Highfolds Scar coming into view. At the brow you can see the tarn below. Descend to the path along the lakeside and turn left. Stride on to pass through the gate and, just beyond, take the wide swathe of grass continuing ahead. This brings you back to the parking area.

Along the way

The high **limestone pastures** through which the path, known as the Monk's Road, passes, were once owned by the monks of Fountains Abbey. They held the fishing rights of Malham Tarn and it is along this Road that mules carried fish from the tarn to Arncliffe for the monks.

The **National Trust** cares for a large area of Malhamdale, stretching from Malham Cove to Fountains Fell, in the heart of the Yorkshire Dales National Park. It manages the reserve in partnership with English Nature and the Field Studies Council. The Trust seeks to balance varied and conflicting interests, including landscape, nature conservation, farming, archaeology and public access. With the help of volunteers, the Trust maintains the footpaths and it also provides information.

The water of **Malham Tarn** contains ancient and rare stoneworts, a wide range of molluscs, white-clawed crayfish and shoals of bullhead. The birdlife seen from the hide on the north shore include waders and wildfowl, including many coot, great crested grebe, tufted duck, mallard and geese.

2
Bordley

Mastiles Lane, where this walk starts, runs through the uplands of Malham Moor, where limestone scars and extensive grassy fells are intermittently enclosed by drystone walls. Youngsters will enjoy this airy way before it turns off to visit the hidden 'township' of Bordley, nestling in a fold in the hills. This quiet corner once supported fifty or more families. Today it has two farmhouses and several well cared for barns.

Start: Parking area just before (west of) Street Gate (GR905656) on Malham Moor.

Total distance: 10.5km (6½ miles)

Height gain: 170m (560ft)

Difficulty: Easy

1 Pass through Street Gate, heading east, to walk the broad track, continuing beside the wall on your right. Descend to a clapper bridge over Gordale Beck to stroll on along the track. Look right, over the wall, to see the great limestone cliffs at the entrance to Gordale Gorge. Carry on to the information board at the site of the Roman Marching Camp and pause here to see if you can spot any trace of the rectangular ditch that surrounded it.

2 Beyond the next gate, notice the line of wire, on the right, just above the wall. The wire, put there to stop the sheep leaping over the wall, is supported by a regular shaped stone rather that a wooden pole that is used nowadays. Continue on through the next gate to walk the wide walled way, rough underfoot in some places. This gradually improves making for pleasing walking. Stroll on to pass through another gate and out onto open pasture, where there is a three-armed signpost.

3 Turn right to walk a wide green swathe of fine sheep-cropped turf, with a wall to your right. Eventually you descend a short reinforced section to come to a four-armed signpost. Go through the wheeled gate, on the right (easy to miss), and ascend the reinforced farm access track to Bordley Green. As the track climbs steadily, enjoy the ever increasing view, over the rock strewn moorland. Then you descend to the delightful hollow in the hilly pastures. Go past the two farmhouses on

9

your right and stroll ahead past a barn on the left. It has a weathervane with a figure of a cow on it similar to those in the fields below, and a plaque with the date 1664. There are lots of footpaths going off from here, but this walk remains on the main track.

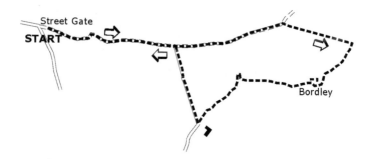

4 Bear right with the track and then left to pass through a gate to climb another good track. Enjoy the extensive view towards Winterburn Reservoir. When the wall on your left turns away carry on along a clear grassy swathe across a field. Then descend the wide grassy buttressed path that descends right to the foot of the lonely, rocky Cow Gill. The way then swings left and climbs upwards past gritstone, to the right, and the pleasing limestone-littered gill to your left. Stroll on the curving way to join a track coming in on the left, and carry on ahead.

5 Continue on the gated way. Where it begins to swing left for Lee Gate Farm, go on ahead for a few steps to pass through a gap-stile beside a gate into a fine walled track. Descend, left, for a short distance towards the start of reinforced Smearbottoms Lane. Here the access track from the farm joins the road. You need to turn right at this point to go through a gate to walk ahead on a signposted track, keeping beside the boundary on your left. Where the track turns left to go through a gate into a pasture, stride on ahead, climbing a little. Then go ahead, still with the wall to your left, to walk a long pasture to reach a gate onto Mastiles Lane. Turn left and walk on to cross the clapper bridge again. The track then takes you on to return to the parking area.

Along the Way

Mastiles Lane Roman Marching Camp is passed early on the walk and on your return. The camp was built during the time that the Romans were campaigning in the north of England. Building the marching camps was all part of a day's work for Roman soldiers. They carried trenching tools, baskets for moving the earth and two wooden stakes as part of their kit. As soon as they came to a halt, at the end of the day's march, men would dig a rectangular ditch and throw up a bank of soil inside it, then place the wooden stakes on top as a palisade. The soldiers slept in leather tents, eight men to a tent, with the commander in this own tent, safe in the middle. The Mastiles Lane Marching camp was probably built during the second half of the first century AD. The Romans were forced to put down a revolt by the Brigantes who controlled much of the north of the country.

At Bordley the **Eshton Beck** starts on its journey to join the River Aire. Here a valley opens out of the moorland and there is a large stretch of open pasture, with farms scattered over it. Beyond their patch of cultivation there lies the moorland ever ready to take over the better land.

While walking the high lonely slopes of the extensive moorland about Bordley, look for and listen for the **curlew**. It is easily recognised by its long, curved bill, which varies from four to seven inches in length. With this it probes the moor for insects and worms. It spends the winter months on the shore, probing the mud for molluscs. It also eats berries.

It has a bulky brown body, which in summer is streaked on the head, back and breast with dark brown and buff. The wings and tail are barred with dark and light brown. Its lower back is white and this makes it easy to recognise in flight.

The curlew makes a poor sort of nest on the ground among stunted heather, crowberry and cotton-grass. Here during April into May it lays three or four large eggs. If you approach a nest (by accident) the bird guarding the young will run towards you, trying to draw you away from the danger zone.

Curlews are gregarious birds; they like to crowd together when feeding on the shore and they nest, several together, but scattered over a patch of moorland. They are noisy birds, delightfully so. Try to recognise the long liquid bubbling calls with which the male communicates with its mate on the nest.

11

3
Above Malham

This walk traverses several very long, wide, grassy tracks or green lanes, leaving you in no doubt where to walk. There is one tiny stretch of road walking and several delightful walled tracks along which you stroll. Youngsters might find the long hill climb a little tedious, but pauses to enjoy retrospective spectacular views and also to realise that they are walking the route taken by those men who worked the mine towards the top of the ridge might encourage them on.

Start: The National Park Visitor Centre car park, Malham (GR900628)

Total distance: 9km (5½ miles)

Height gain: 300m (985ft)

Difficulty: Mostly easy except for the steepish climb below Pikedaw Hill

1 Leave the car park and turn right into a hedged track. A few steps along, wind right, and walk for 300m to turn left onto another pleasing stony, green lane, signed Pikedaw. From here there are superb views, to the right, of Malham Cove. Carry on until you reach a Y-junction, just beyond the small water treatment works. Continue on the left branch to pass several fine field barns. Step across a narrow ford or use the small clapper bridge, on the left. Just beyond, climb the gated step-stile over the wall, on the right. Beyond, walk ahead to the corner of two walls, where you need to cross a plank bridge over a stream. Stroll ahead towards another field barn (Butterlands Barn) and climb the gated step-stile over the wall just beyond it.

2 Cross a small stream and turn right to begin your steady climb, on a distinct green swathe of short grass. The way winds a little to the left before reaching a waymarked gated step-stile, below the limestone slopes of Pikedaw Hill. Go on up the clear way with rolling hillocks, drumlins, to your left. Carry on with a tumbledown wall to your right. After a short steep climb, slightly left, the path levels and the grassy swathe continues to another stile. Just before it, walk a few steps, right, into a little valley to see a beautifully constructed entrance to an adit

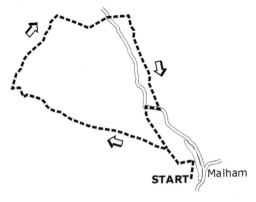

START Malham

or disused horizontal shaft. Before climbing the stile, energetic young people might like to ascend right, keeping beside the wall on the left, then at the brow winding right to the cairn on top of Pikedaw (430m/ 1398ft).

3 Climb the stile and walk on for half a mile, ignoring any right turns, over the high moorland. Watch out for your first view of Malham Tarn. When you can spot, ahead, a farm gate and a prominent signpost in a transverse wall, continue on any path that leads to it. Go through the gate and turn right to walk a clear grassy way. Where the wall turns away right, note the Nappa Cross (a small pillar of dressed stone, fixed to the wall corner). Here leave the wall and descend, slightly left, on the grassy way to a gate in the wall below.

4 Beyond, descend steadily through rough pastures, to go through two more gates and on down to a signpost, just before a wall. Turn right and continue on a slightly rougher but still grassy track. Follow it for half-a-mile and then wind left, with it, to join the fell road. Cross, climb the stile and walk down a grassy path, with the wall to your left. Just before the ladder-stile, turn right, climb a little slope to walk a clear path, beside a fence on your left, from where there is a fine view of the magical limestone Dry Valley (see Walk 4).

5 The path leads to a ladder-stile onto Ewe Moor and continues on an easy-to-follow wide green trod. At a cross of tracks, keep ahead and go through a derelict wall and then take three more ladder-stiles; from the last you can see Malham Cove curving away to the left, below you. Carry on where the open access land ceases, remaining on the footpath as it swings right and winds on, arriving at a gate onto the fell road once more. Cross and stroll right for a few steps to the corner of the road, to take on the left, a gate to a field path, signed Malham 1 mile.

13

6 As you walk, enjoy more dramatic views, and then follow the path as it leads to a gate into another walled lane (Long Lane). Continue on to pass the water treatment works, now on your left, and go ahead to the T-junction of tracks. Turn right and walk on until you can curve left. A few steps along the car park lies to your left.

Along the way

Malham village lies near the head of its own dale, which is barely 5 miles/8km long. It is a spectacular five miles of classic limestone scenery. On this walk you pass vast sheets of limestone pavement and mile after mile of criss-crossing drystone walls, which contrast sharply, and pleasingly, with the bright green grass. Many of the pastures have a fine field barn, built to store winter feed for cattle. Once trees would have covered the lower slopes of the dale except for the limestone pavements and the hilltops. Today ash, bird cherry, and some oak and birch, crowd the steep slopes of the gills and anywhere that is inaccessible to hungry sheep.

Malham was once a centre for great sheep fairs. Two abbeys, Fountains and Bolton, had granges in the dale. Fountains owned or leased over a million acres in the Craven uplands. Granges were high-level grazing grounds for livestock. Sheep farming was an important occupation that brought a good income for the monks. They transported the wool from the outlying granges by trains of packhorses. These took the most direct route, whatever hill etc was in the way (even over the top of Penyghent). As they journeyed back and forth they made tracks over the moors, for example the Monk's Road (see Walk 1). These were often 'waymarked' with a monastic cross (see Walk 4), and you pass a restored Nappa Cross on the wall in Point 3 above. Later they were believed to have been used as preaching stones.

Take care when you peep down at the delightful entrance to the adit or horizontal shaft. Very often coal or mineral workings were troubled with drainage and a shaft had to be constructed to draw off the water.

4
Janet's Foss, Gordale Scar, Malham Cove

This walk takes you first to Janet's Foss. Janet was believed to be Queen of the local fairies. 'Foss' is the Norse word for waterfall. Legend has it that Janet lived in the small cave behind the dramatic fall, where Gordale Beck makes a spectacular descent. The route continues into the deep narrow gorge that leads to the waterfalls of Gordale Scar. After passing through more spectacular limestone scenery you return to the magnificent pavement on the top of Malham Cove. Steps take you down to the valley below from where you can really appreciate the splendid 100m high amphitheatre of rock.

Start: Pay-and-display car park at Malham. (GR900628)

Total distance: 10.5km (6½ miles)

Height gain: 180m (590ft)

Difficulty: Generally good paths and tracks.

Challenging where some sections of the paths are rough underfoot. After rain the Dry Valley and the limestone pavement can be very slippery. Take care with very young children as you cross the limestone pavement – though if you hug the right-hand edge you can just about keep them away from the clints and grikes, and the sudden drop to the valley below.

Do not attempt this walk in the poor visibility.

1 Cross the road from the car park and walk left to take a footbridge (in summer quite hidden by overhanging vegetation) across Malham Beck, opposite the River House Hotel. Turn right and follow the clearly signposted gated track to Mires Barn. Go left here and follow the well waymarked, reinforced path through several gates and then into pleasing ancient deciduous woodland. Take care as you walk over the tree roots and continue to the foot of Janet's Foss. After a delightful pause, carry on up the rough path to a narrow lane, where you turn right.

2 Pass, on your left, a picturesque old bridge and go on to a gate on the left. Beyond, walk the sturdy track through the immense, dramatic, dark gorge to come to the base of the

15

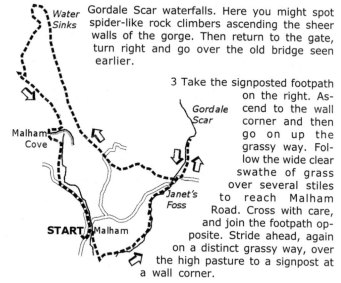

Gordale Scar waterfalls. Here you might spot spider-like rock climbers ascending the sheer walls of the gorge. Then return to the gate, turn right and go over the old bridge seen earlier.

3 Take the signposted footpath on the right. Ascend to the wall corner and then go on up the grassy way. Follow the wide clear swathe of grass over several stiles to reach Malham Road. Cross with care, and join the footpath opposite. Stride ahead, again on a distinct grassy way, over the high pasture to a signpost at a wall corner.

4 Bear slightly right to a stile over the wall ahead to continue through a narrow limestone valley that children will enjoy exploring. Beyond the next stile, at the head of the valley, carry on along another wide grassy swathe. Where the way soon divides, keep to the right branch. This leads you on and then winds right, and then left, round three murky pools. Continue on to come to a signpost. Here stroll on (left) along a narrower path in the direction of 'Water Sinks'. The path winds round a hillock and then descends to a gated stile over a wall. Beyond a signpost directs you left.

5 Stroll another wide grassy swathe beside the wall. Take care over a rough, rocky section and then go on over more grass. Then head on along the clear path that runs along the side of the deep Dry Valley to your left. Follow the way as it winds round right, high above a spectacular limestone hollow. Stroll the continuing terraced path that winds on and leads to a double stile on your left.

6 Beyond, now doubling back under the terrace-like path, go down a rocky staircase through a limestone wonderland. At the foot, stroll the clear path through the valley viewed from above. Go through one of two stiles and wind on round, on the

path, for a short distance to arrive at the edge of the famous limestone pavement at the top of Malham Cove.

7 Wind right and step, with care, from clint to clint. Pause on a flattish stone if you wish to look down into the grykes to enjoy the wonderful variety of plants growing in the sheltered environment. Or, find your way to the right of the pavement where progress, onwards, might be easier for younger children. At the end of the pavement you reach a wall. Bear left for a few steps to go through a kissing-gate at the top of a long flight of steps.

8 Then begin the descent of the wide easy steps, which wind down a very long way to the valley bottom. Turn left and continue for as far as the water level allows to enjoy the grandeur of this magnificent amphitheatre, and to see a stream flowing out of the base of the huge cliff. Here again you might like to watch the rock climbers.

9 Then return along the path and walk on with the beck to your left, along the signposted way to join a road. Turn left and descend the narrow road, with care (no pavement). Walk on into the village of Malham. The car park lies at the far end.

Along the Way

At **Janet's Foss**, lime-rich water descends over the mossy edge of the fall. Calcite is deposited and the moss becomes petrified, forming an apron of rock, from the lip to the plunge pool, and known as a tufa screen.

Gordale Beck rises on the lonely moorland above Bordley. It then descends through a dramatic limestone gorge to the top of the waterfalls at Gordale Scar. Once a narrow deep lake filled this high level ravine, but in 1730, a violent flood broke through the debris at its foot and water gushed forth. Today if you stand below the fall you might be able to see the beck high above, spouting through the jagged hole in the limestone.

Malham Beck flows out of the glacially formed Malham Tarn. Once it hurried down the Dry Valley and then tumbled over Malham Cove to the lovely green valley below. Today, Malham Beck disappears below ground at Water Sinks and reappears at Aire Head Springs. It has been proven by using chemicals in the water that the stream seen coming out of the foot of the Cove is not Malham Beck but another stream rising on Malham Moor.

The **limestone edge** of the pavement above Malham Cove appears quite suddenly. This is because though the limestone is pervious to water it is very hard. On the pavement itself, care is needed as the limestone slabs (clints) are separated by fissures (grikes) that can be very deep or quite shallow. In the grikes look for lowly plants thriving in the cool depths of the crevices well protected from hungry sheep.

Just recently more than 50 tons of walling stones were airlifted by helicopter to the top of Malham Cove to construct a new section of wall. A new gate was also built, which replaced two steep ladder-stiles that had to be climbed before.

As you walk you might be lucky to spot a brown shape diving into some twisted dried grass. This will probably be a **short-tailed vole** once called a grass mouse, field mouse or field vole. It is a stumpy creature with a blunt oval head and tiny round ears just protruding from its fur. It has a short rather stiff tail. It can be found in almost every habitat from meadows and damp pastures to woodland and mountain tops. It feeds on almost anything vegetable and it also consumes large numbers of insects.

The female makes her nest among dried grass litter. She gives birth after 21days and the young are blind and naked at birth. There may be five, six, or seven in a litter, with several litters in a season from late February to September. The young are weaned at 14 to 18 days, and are mature at three weeks. They mate at six weeks of age. Why are we not over-run by them? Because they are predated by owls, weasels, rooks, kestrels buzzards, harriers and foxes.

You might also spot a **fox** on this walk. They have been seen hurrying through grikes when they have been disturbed by walkers moving over the clints.

5
Malham, Kirkby Malham, Weets Top

On a summer's day the car park at Malham can become full and vehicles spill out onto the road. This walk leaves the hurly-burly of the little village by a stile opposite the visitor centre and soon walkers are well away from the bustle. Almost immediately you pass Aire Head, barely noticeable, but here the Aire starts and continues on through lovely countryside before eventually becoming wide and almost unrecognisable as it passes through industrial towns on its way to join the River Ouse.

Start: The Visitor Centre, Malham (GR900628)

Total distance: 10.5km (6½ miles)

Height gain: 280m (920ft)

Difficulty: Moderate. Easy path alongside the River Aire. Steepish narrow road climb through Hanlith. Steady moorland climb to Weets Top on an indistinct grassy swathe.

1 Cross the road from the visitor centre and take the gap-stile, signed 'Hanlith Bridge 1 mile'. Walk on over the pasture, keeping parallel with the long wall on your left, beyond which flows Malham Beck. Pass through a kissing-gate in the far left corner and in a few steps cross Tanpits footbridge. Then cross a track to go through a kissing-gate and walk ahead to climb a gated stile. Beyond, look down, left, to see water (in summer) oozing out under a turf and trickling on to join the Malham Beck. The united waters become the River Aire. Climb the next ladder-stile and carry on to go past a seat.

2 The path leads on along the edge of a leat, where shallow water is contained in a regular, long, concrete channel. *Here young children should be under close control.* Beyond, down a slope, left and almost hidden by trees and dense undergrowth, flows the silvery Aire. Weave between intriguing low walls of the leat and then the reason for it becomes apparent – Scalegill Mill. This was a cotton mill built in the late 18th century. It used the water of the River Aire to provide power for its spinning machines, first using a waterwheel and then water driven turbines. The mill closed in 1991 and was

19

converted into a complex of dwellings and the leat is now ornamental. Walk on along the right side of the mill to pass through a gap-stile.

3 Just beyond, join a reinforced track and then leave it immediately to take a rising green swathe, climbing right to a gap-stile in the wall on Cock Thorns Hill (180m/590ft). Continue on the clear path, climbing slightly to go over a step-stile at a wall. Continue on the diagonal path all the way to another step-stile, which decants you onto a road. Cross and walk left and then wind, with great care, round the left-hand bend. A short distance along go through the large wooden gates (easy-to-miss) part of the lych-gate into the churchyard of Kirkby Malham's, St Michael the Archangel. As you near the church, notice the gate on the left signed 'Watery Grave' – see below. After pausing in the church leave by the top gate and turn left.

4 Walk past the Victoria Inn. Cross the Malham Road, with care, and continue ahead along Green Gate, signed 'Hanlith Only'. Stroll past some delightful cottages and carry on as it winds left and then right to cross the River Aire. Continue on the narrow lane as it begins to climb through the hamlet, passing fine Hanlith Hall on your right. Remain on the lane as it zigzags upwards, easing the gradient, until it ceases to be tarmacked.

5 Carry on the walled track. Look across the lovely valley (left) for a fine view of Malham Cove, and then follow the way where it winds a little to the right and then left. The signposted track ends at a gate through which you pass. Ascend a short rough track, reinforced with boulders and, where this ceases, carry on ahead over a peaty area, soon to join an indistinct path continuing up towards The Weets. After three-quarters of a mile on the narrow path, a couple of waymarks are passed and guide you to the corner of two

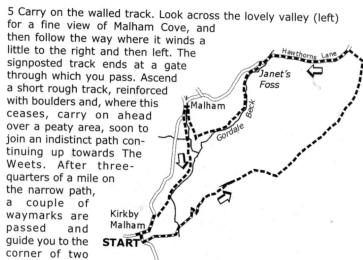

20

walls. Go through a gate and walk to the nearby signpost.

6 Follow the direction for 'Weets Top ¼ mile', heading towards the next signpost, where you join a wide bridlepath and turn left. From here you can see the top of Ingleborough. Head on to the next signpost to follow the direction arm for 'Hawthorns Lane ¼ mile'. (First you may like to walk on a short distance to the trig point against the wall.) Go through the gate and before you start your descent of the gated, rough track, look left to see the remains of a monastic cross, a 'waymarker' to help travellers over the moors (see Walk 4), and possibly a boundary marker.

7 At Hawthorns Lane, turn left and walk on to the valley bottom. Pass, on the right, the gate to Gordale Scar and a few steps along turn left into a footpath signed Janet's Foss. Take the right branch and take care as you descend the limestone rocks, part of the path that can be slippery, to come to the pool at the foot of the pretty waterfall. After a pause here continue on through gated woodland and meadows to arrive at a barn. Follow the waymarked path, right, to return to Malham. Cross the footbridge in the centre of the village and turn left to return to the visitor centre.

Along the Way

Go through the gate in **Kirkby Malham's churchyard**, marked 'Watery Grave', to find a small stream. Here a tale is told of a loving wife, separated for most of the year from her husband who worked abroad, for much of her married life. Before she died she asked to be buried on the other side of water – the stream – from her husband. He died first and, alas, when the wife came to be buried the gravediggers found that the other side of the stream was solid rock. Both were buried in the same grave.

The **church of Kirkby Malham** stands on the site of a pre-Conquest foundation. The present church was entirely rebuilt in the 15th century. It is wonderfully spacious, and with its fine oak roof and its other features may remind visitors of churches in Norfolk. The reason for this? The Abbey of West Dereham, in Norfolk, held the benefice of St Michael's from the 12th century until the reformation. Skilful restoration in the 1880 retained its air of medieval beauty.

All around Malham, in spectacular limestone country, are **pot-holes and caves**, and the five great hills, Penyghent,

Ingleborough, Whernside, and Great and Little Whernside. A clear bubbling stream, Malham Beck, divides the stone houses of the village, some of which are white-washed cottages with roses growing round the doors. These share the village with a few shops, two inns, B&Bs, a hotel and a national park centre.

As you walk this route, note the change in the colour of the walls on Weets Top and those close to Gordale Scar and Malham Cove. The reason is that between the gritstone scenery on top of the moor and the limestone scenery, barely a mile away, lies the Mid Craven Fault as one of the great geological upheavals is named.

The parish registers in the church at Kirkby Malham show two signatures purporting to be those of Oliver Cromwell – on January 17 and July 25, 1655 – as a witness at two village weddings. Cromwell's trusted officer, General Lambert, lived at nearby Calton Hall and it is possible that Cromwell might have visited his good friend on those dates. But it is doubted that Cromwell would have ventured north in the winter for the January wedding and on July 24 and 26, the days before and after the supposed signing, he attended special meetings in London.

Harry J. Scott, in his fascinating book 'Portrait of Yorkshire', suggests that the signatures might be a practical joke or that the parish clerk needed a name and added Cromwell's. Thomas Carlyle, the author of a life of Cromwell, says that Cromwell's supposed signature in the register bears no resemblance to his genuine one and doubted that such a great statesman would witness a village wedding.

6
Airton to Bell Busk

This walk takes you along the Pennine Way from the pretty village of Airton, over grassy Eshton Moor and on to Bell Busk. The route runs, for much of the way, close beside the River Aire, here quite narrow as it passes through delightful rolling pastures and water meadows. The return is along Kirk Syke Lane, a delightful track that runs through large cultivated fields and woodland. This ramble makes an ideal start for youngsters attempting their first walk through quiet, sparsely populated countryside using mainly level paths and tracks.

Start: A lay-by for three or four cars beyond the bridge over the River Aire at the foot of the village of Airton (GR903594)

Total distance: 7.4km (4½ miles)

Height gain: 120m (363ft)

Difficulty: Any ascents are very gradual. If the Aire has burst its shallow banks, there are diversionary paths along the Pennine Way. In high summer, the thistles on Eshton Moor can be rather tiresome.

1 From the lay-by beyond the bridge, cross the road to take a signposted gap to steps down into the meadow beyond, and walk on with the river to your right. Carry on along the grassy swathe to climb a gated stile. Go on ahead, curving right, with a wall to your right, to take the step-stile over a wall. Continue on along the riverside at the edge of a large pasture and then swing slightly left to take a stile over the wall, ahead, under a tree. Turn right and cross the bridge over the Aire and then turn left to walk a few steps to an unsigned stile on your left.

2 Bear right to walk with the river, now to your left, along a clear path. Cross a little plank bridge and continue on with a wall to your right and forest trees beyond. Then when the river bars your way, take the step-stile onto a low wall, on your right, and continue on the wall, just above the hurrying water. *Small children should be under close control here*. Then the path continues at the foot of a steep slope (can be muddy in the winter) densely covered with trees. Go through the next gate and walk on beside the river, with a wall to your right. Pass under a mixed deciduous copse, with the River Aire still to your left

23

3 Stroll on to cross the river, now very narrow here, by a footbridge. Pause awhile to enjoy this pretty corner. Follow the path as it winds left and then right to a signposted step-stile.

Walk right up a slope, with the narrow road to your left beyond a fence, to come to a signpost. Follow the grassy way, which ascends a huge pasture. Pause often to look back at the delightful view, and go on to come to another signpost. From the signpost, make an acute right turn to go through a small signposted gate into a large pasture, closely covered with thistles. Bear half right and walk across the pasture to pass through a purpose-built gap in the wall.

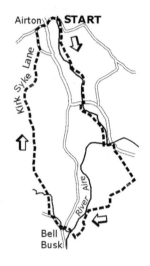

4 Turn left and walk parallel with the wall – there are fewer thistles here. Remain beside the wall to eventually join a well-used wide grassy track that, after passing through another gap in the wall, drops diagonally down to a gate where several walls meet. Beyond the gate, walk down a field beside a wall on your left. Pass High Laithe barn and go on to pass through the next gate. Continue descending to come near to the River Aire. Wind left with the wall and walk on along another grassy way to come to a gate. Beyond follow the track behind a farmhouse and then between outbuildings. Carry on the way as it winds right and continues to a T-junction of tracks. Turn right and walk on to cross Aire Bridge.

5 Head on to cross another bridge over Kirk Syke Beck, which soon unites with the Aire. At the end of this bridge, turn right in the direction of Bell Busk. Walk on along the lane and just before a house named Raven Flatt, take a bridleway on the right. At first the track passes through an enormous amount of discarded machinery, cars and other dumped material. Go through a gate and out on to a reinforced way into the open countryside. Cross a stone bridge over Kirk Syke Beck and go by a barn, with a waymark on its corner and a notice asking walkers and riders to keep beside the fence on the left.

6 After a gentle climb this brings you to a signposted gate.

Beyond turn right and walk along the side of a pasture to go through the next gate. Walk on towards a barn, Well Head Laithe, where you continue to the left of it, passing through a shady copse. Go through another gate, soon to continue along a walled track. After the next gate walk on up a hedged track. Go past a barn and then on along a reinforced track. Carry on past a huge barn and then on along the track shaded by very tall trees.

7 At the road, turn left and at the T-junction, go on down the lane, to reach the bridge over the Aire and the lay-by, beyond.

Along the way

After you have crossed the main road on your return through Airton, you pass, on your right, **Airton Quaker Hostel**. The Meeting House was built by William Ellis in 1690 and it is still used for worship. The adjoining hostel was originally the stable for the Quakers attending meetings.

As you descend to cross the bridge on your return from the walk, look left to see two long plain buildings. The nearest from where you are standing was originally a corn mill. In 1787 the furthest building was built to spin cotton. In 1825 Isaac and John Dewhurst took over the mill and ran it until it ceased production in 1904. In 1918 the mill was sold to an engineering firm which supplied the first electricity to houses in Airton. In 1972, the Airton Mill was sold as one unit and converted into apartments.

The **Pennine Way** runs for 256 miles along the 'backbone' of England, dividing the east from the west of the country. Much of the Way provides tough walking, over lonely moorland, across boggy and misty high ground. The first part of this walk is along a very gentle section of the Way, close beside a charming river and unless the Aire floods not through any bogs.

7
Calton, Weets Top, Winterburn Reservoir

The moorland is always broodingly near on this walk. Complete this ramble when youngsters are old enough to appreciate the wide open rolling spaces, the air is full of birdsong and not-so-common flowers dot the way. Choose a spring or summer's day to fully appreciate the charm of this walk.

Start: Park carefully without blocking anyone's access in the 'dead end road' about which cluster the attractive houses of the tiny hamlet of Calton. (GR909593)

Total distance: 13km (8 miles)

Height gain: 210m (693ft)

Difficulty: Slow steady climb to Weets Top and then a glorious descent to Winterburn Reservoir. Pleasing tracks then take you on to less clear footpaths across the moor.

1 Walk ahead along the road to its end and then go on ahead on a clear, walled track, signed Weets Top. If the ford is too deep, look for the footbridge to the right (as it is half a tree trunk it might be slippery after rain). Walk on, gradually climbing through the woodland of Foss Gill, with the unseen beck tumbling in noisy falls. Go through two gates onto the open moorland.

2 Follow the continuing good track as it zigzags before climbing steadily uphill. Soon a wall comes in on your left and you keep parallel with it all the way to the top. The track is grassy in many places, but there are some boggy patches after rain. Beyond the first stile, a good path continues, reinforced and slightly raised above the boggy environs on either side. As you go, watch for short-eared owls that drift just above the vegetation hunting, silently, for prey. You might also spot a 'flittery' bird, a snipe, taking off from the ooze.

3 Go past the first signpost encountered and stroll on a short distance to Weets Top, where there is a trig point against the wall, just after the gate on the left. Turn right here, following the signpost for Hetton. Stride another pleasing, shorter, grassy swathe over the moorland to go through the gate

ahead. Turn right and walk on along a good trod beside the wall on your right. Follow it as both wall and track curve left. Then wind right with the wall as it begins to descend. A short way down the track, now solidly reinforced and raised, it swings, left, across the lower moorland.

4 Go through a gap in the wall, descend a short rough path to ford a stream and then walk on along the excellent way across the moorland. Go through the next gate and follow the good path as it winds right across a pasture. At the time of writing (2005) it suddenly ends. Go on along the continuing grassy swathe and where it soon winds left to a signpost by a gate.

5 Beyond, stroll the distinct way through rushy pasture to go

through the next gate and then follow the grassy trod downhill to arrive at a signposted gate, just before a Water Board bridge over the outflow from Winterburn Reservoir. Go through the gate, on the right, in the direction of Winterburn. Cross a small ford and climb a ladder-stile. Continue ahead, through a meadow, beside a wall on the left. As you near the reservoir, look for geese and ducks idling on the water. Pass through a gate and then down two steps to cross a bridge of sleepers over a little stream and climb the slope beyond. Stroll on beside the reservoir fence until you are forced to turn right before a deep gill. Keep along the field edge to climb the step-stile onto a narrow access road.

6 Turn left and follow the road as it crosses a narrow inlet from the reservoir and, at the top of the little slope, take the signposted stile on the right. Walk ahead up a large pasture, aiming for the left side of Way Gill farmhouse. Just before the dwelling, go through a signposted gate on your left. Walk ahead to join the farm's signposted access track. Turn left and walk on through the charming quiet countryside. A short distance along, take the right turn, a signposted track, to Cowper Cote. Follow the reinforced track and where it swings left and continues on to pass a house on the left. Go through a gate and walk ahead on a good track, with a fence to your right. Continue where it winds right and passes through another gate. Carry on beside the wall on your right to go through a broken gate. Walk on, watching for a ladder-stile on your right, which you climb. Turn left and walk down a slope to step across a small stream, with woodland to your right. Climb the slope to go over the next ladder-stile onto the moorland.

7 Walk ahead to pass to the right of a dilapidated barn, which was once very fine, and then wind, a little left, round its end to take a clear but narrow path going on ahead. Go through a gateless gap and walk on along a narrow path. To your left is a ditch and a fence and a scraggly row of hawthorns. Half way along the path, it continues on an embanked way, possibly the top of an old wall.

8 Just before the corner of this large moorland pasture, follow a very short path, diagonally right, to go through a gate. Walk ahead on a clear grassy swathe, still over the moorland, to a gate in the wall ahead. Beyond, follow the clear green track as it climbs gently and then winds left, round a hillock, to walk down the middle of a pasture in the direction of the solidly built

gritstone farmhouse, Cowper Cote. Swing right before it to go through a gate. Stride on along the narrow path as it drifts a little right and drops down to a stile, over a fence below a gnarled ash. Then head up the field, in the same general direction, towards a barn. Climb the ladder-stile on its far side and walk on ahead to climb an unusual wooden stile. Walk on ahead, with a fence to your right, to climb a similar stile.

9 Go on beside a wall, on your left, to pass through a gate to a farm track. This can be very, very muddy. Follow the track into Calton, where you turn left to rejoin your car.

Along the way

Richard I, in AD 1200, confirmed that land had been given by the son of Alan de Calton, to the monks of Fountains, Dereham and Bolton. On the dissolution of the religious houses these lands were acquired by John Lambert.

Calton nestles in the Yorkshire Dales near to Kirkby Malham. For years it was the 'seat of power' for the Lambert family. The most famous was Major General John Lambert, the great grandson of the original John. He was known and respected as Oliver Cromwell's second in command and in this position he found wealth and power.

After the downfall of Cromwell, and the restoration of the monarchy, the Major General was sentenced to perpetual exile in Guernsey. His forfeited estates were granted to Lord Fauconberg who in turn sold them another John Lambert, son of the General. During his lifetime the very large old building burnt down and was replaced by a hall-like mansion. The church at Kirkby Malham has many items relating to the Lambert family including the Lambert memorial.

The **Winterburn Reservoir** was built around 1892 to provide water for the Leeds and Liverpool Canal in times of shortage. A 9-mile pipeline carries the water to the outlet just above the lock keeper's cottage, which stands beside the middle lock at Greenberfield.

8
Hetton

Children will enjoy this delightful walk along two pleasing walled lanes. The climb up over a small part of the moor will present quite a challenge and perhaps several pauses will help all the family to arrive at the top. The return down Moor Lane can almost be skipped.

Start: Hetton. Park in a quiet road, making sure not to block anyone's drive or gate. (GR962588)

Total distance: 7.3km (4½ miles)

Height gain: 80m (260ft)

Difficulty: All easy walking except for the climb up to Long Hill farm and that is not too difficult for all ages.

1 From where you have parked, take the signposted bridleway, Moor Lane, which lies a short distance, north-east of the Angel Inn, Hetton. This wide, walled track, well-reinforced and easy-to-walk, stretches ahead, climbing a little and passing through fertile fields. After nearly three-quarters of a mile, turn left into another wide, walled way, Cross Lane, which is more grassy than Moor Lane. As you descend gently, extensive views open up of walled and hedged fields. Away to the left stretches a dramatic ridge of fells. Go past a field barn and then through a gate across the lane. Beyond, is glorious wall-to-wall soft green turf along which you continue. Follow the lane as it winds right and passes, on the left, Owslin, once a fine small house but now used as a byre. Carry on this short piece of track to come to a gate.

2 Go through the gate, turn right and walk a few steps across the pasture to go through a gate in the wall. From here climb up the moorland hill for just over half a mile. As you go keep roughly parallel with walls to your left to arrive at the topmost left-hand wall corner. Pass through and walk ahead over rough pasture following helpful posts that mark the path. To your left lie several dwellings. Take the next gate through a wall and go on to pass Long Hill farm. Go on ahead through the next gate and then walk the little path, waymarked, with rushy pasture close on either side.

3 Pass through the next gate into a shelterbelt of trees. To

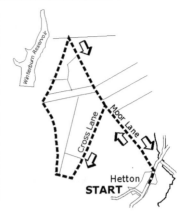

emerge from this narrow strip of woodland you may have to go into the trees on the left and step over the fence, where other walkers have done so, if you find the gate (waymarked) too difficult to open. Walk ahead on a grassy swathe to a signposted gate onto Moor Lane. Turn right and begin you steady descent on the gated way back to Hetton. Turn right at the busy road and go past the Angel Inn to where you have parked.

Along the way

You will see many **sheep** on this walk. They are undemanding animals. They will nibble happily at anything in a pasture and graze it to the ground. They have to be hardy enough to withstand the cold and wet winter. Apart from the Herdwick, the Swaledale is the hardiest of all British sheep. It has an important role as a crossing breed, the mother of such hybrids as the Mule and Masham. Many of the great abbeys of Yorkshire grew rich from the wool clipped from their great flocks.

You may wonder why the sheep you pass on the moorland do not get lost and cannot be found by the farmer on his quad bike or by his dog. These sheep have a strong homing instinct, which keeps them on their own land or 'heaf'. They are always kept on their own land even though the ownership of the farm might change.

The many fine **walls** around Hetton were built to enclose grazing land. The field barns were used to store hay and house cattle during the winter. The cows spent the summer in the fields and then in November were moved into the barns. Twice a day the farmer would visit all his barns to feed the cattle from the stored hay and to milk them. He would remove the dung that dropped into a channel. Today, cattle are housed near the farm and the barns are rarely used.

31

9
Otterburn

This is one of the shorter walks in this book. It is a delight for all its route. Youngsters will enjoy the differing environments and adults will appreciate that there is only a tiny stretch of road walking. In spring, when the moorland is home to nesting curlews, wheatears, skylarks and meadow pipits, it is a joy to walk. The tiny Wenningber Wood plays host to small songbirds and even the rather formidable plantation, to the right of Dacre Lane, is frequented by the colourful bullfinch.

Start: The hamlet of Otterburn (GR883575). Make sure you do not obstruct farm gates or entrances to houses.

Total distance: 8km (5 miles)

Height gain: 160m (525ft)

Difficulty: Mainly on good tracks which might be muddy in places after rain. The paths over the airy moor are faint but mainly dry and easy. If Crook Beck is in spate, where it crosses under Dacre Lane, you will have to return. Choose a good day.

1 Start the walk up signposted Dacre Lane (track). This leaves, west, of the tiny hamlet on the north side of the narrow road to Hellifield. Climb the pleasing walled way, lined with forest trees and with fields on either side, beyond. Then the trees of a large conifer plantation, fronted to the lane by oak, crowd in on the right. At the top of the slope go through a gate, with the small Wenningber Wood to your left, where the Woodland Trust welcomes you. Here you might spot bullfinches flitting across the track.

2 Go through the next gate, leaving the woodland behind. Ascend the wide grassy way, keeping to the right of a small copse of Scots pine, ash and oak. Just above the trees Crook Beck flows from a spring. To the left of the trees rises Butter Haw (267m/865ft). Go through the gate at the top of the grassy hillock and walk on along a good track to pass through the next gate. This leads out into much rougher pasture, where some Highland cattle graze. Go through the next gate and stroll a walled track that is muddy. Fortunately there is a drier grassy path to the right of the track. Then the track itself becomes grassy and descends to a signpost.

3 Turn right here, in the direction of 'Ebor Gate' and go through the gate, or climb the ladder-stile, into more rough pasture, sheltered by low hills on either side. Walk on ahead along a narrow grassy path, through rushes, keeping parallel with the wall on your right. Ignore a wide track that leads uphill, left, and go on ahead still in line with the wall on your right. Go through a gateless gap. Carry on towards a shelterbelt of deciduous trees ahead. Step across a little beck and head steadily half right. Go through a gate and on over a sturdy step-stile. Cross the next little stream (the infant Otterburn Beck) and then with the shelterbelt of trees to your left, climb a grassy swathe, keeping equidistant between the wall away to your left and that to your right.

4 At the top of the slope the path becomes two. Keep to the left branch. Carry on over the moorland pasture to come to a narrow stream passing through a grassy gill. Descend and climb up the other side and head on an indistinct way towards the wall ahead, where you go over a good solid step-stile. Beyond, cross a large sheep pasture, bearing slightly left to reach a gate in the far left corner. Beyond, join a good reinforced track and turn right. Wind round the back of pretty Orms Gill Green where, on the left, opposite the dwelling, is a splendid lime kiln. Then carry on along the reinforced Orms Gill Green Lane. As you continue enjoy the fine views across this lovely, more gentle, corner of the Dales. Look for the small covered reservoir in the field on your right.

5 Then take the unsigned gate on your right, just before the next wall. Walk ahead beside the wall on your left. Wind right to the corner of the transverse wall and here turn left to pass through a gate onto rough sheep pasture. As you descend

towards the left corner, join a track that leads down to a gate. Pause to enjoy this attractive corner where the Otterburn Beck slides along a gill, with a wall to its right, before passing through the wall and hurrying on through a pleasing wooded area.

6 Beyond the gate, walk on along the continuing reinforced track, past tiny Park House with its enormous barn. Carry on the pleasing way through deciduous woodland and then go through a gate into a large pasture. Continue with the beck away to the right. Ignore the next gate and remain in the pasture, walking beside the wall on your right, to reach a signposted gate on the right onto a good track, with the beck to your right once more. Stroll on the delightful way, with deciduous woodland over the wall to your left. The track leads to the right of a dwelling and then goes on through large ornate iron gates onto a narrow road in the middle of Otterburn. From here walk on to where you have parked.

Along the way

Wenningber Plantation lies approximately 180m (600ft) above sea level to the north-west of Otterburn village. It is sheltered by Wenningber Hill and is accessed from Dacre Lane. It is typical of small woodlands that were planted across the Yorkshire Dales in the 19th century, on otherwise unusable ground, and in this case very wet ground. Scots pine and sycamore were planted first and it was hoped these trees would give some timber and shelter for stock.

Crook Beck crosses its north-west corner and ditches have been dug to drain water into the beck. The beck then passes under Dacre Lane and into the sitka spruce plantation opposite, eventually to add its water to the Otterburn Beck.

The little plantation was purchased by the Woodland Trust (WT) in 1990. By that time the walls and stock fences were in a poor state and sheep had sheltered beneath trees (one of the original purposes for planting the wood) and grazed the understorey and the ground flora. By 1991, the walls and stock fences were restored and oak, ash, cherry, rowan, hawthorn, alder, hazel and birch were planted. These were protected by various 'sleeves'. The trees are still small considering their age as they suffer from the high altitude and exposure to the moorland weather.

Access to the little wood is freely available, but the overgrown drains make it very difficult to walk – better to just look. Don't forget that during very wet weather the ford, where Crook Beck is culverted under the lane (not at all obvious normally), becomes impassable.

The first you might see of a pair of bullfinches are their white rumps as they flit across the track in front of you. The red breast feathers of the male sometimes reveals where it is perched in a conifer tree on the edge of a forest ride. Close by will be the female, a much browner bird, but with the same large head. It is believed that they pair for life and keep in touch with a soft clear call that sounds like 'whib, whib'. In winter they come into gardens after buds and seeds. They are very partial to the seeds of the sycamore. They pick up the keys and turn them round in their large bills to devour the seed within.

Several of the walks in this book take you through, or close to, woodland and this provides youngsters with a good opportunity to begin to identify trees by their leaves, shape and buds and by where they grow. Pause in Wenningber Plantation and try to identify the more common trees. The very tall trees with needle-thin leaves are most likely to be **Scots Pine**. These shed some of their leaves for much of the year and you probably enjoyed walking the track covered with them. They soften the hardness of the ground and deaden the sound of your boots. They are coniferous trees. They lose only a few leaves at a time and they remain green all year round. Each needle has a hard outer layer and this stops the tree from losing too much water, when essential water for growth from the ground might be frozen.

Sycamores are deciduous trees and they shed their large leaves in the autumn in order to avoid losing precious water. If you are walking in summer look for large bunches of green winged seeds called 'keys'; these turn papery brown in autumn and begin to fall off. The keys get picked up by the wind and get carried well away from the parent tree in order to start growing in the next year as a small seedling. These are the keys so attractive to bullfinches. Sycamores have been planted to provide shelter belts for exposed buildings. Look for them as you cross the pastures towards several farms.

10
Gargrave and Sharp Haw

This last walk should be attempted when you think the young-sters in the family are ready for a real challenge. The walk along the towpath of the Leeds and Liverpool Canal, especially in summer, is full of interest, where you can watch narrow boats negotiating the Gargrave locks or keep a watchful eye for the flash of blue of a kingfisher. Then comes a long steady climb, on two quiet, shady lanes. Once onto the high-level common the views are stupendous and the dramatic top of Sharp Haw beckons, entices, all walkers. The return from the top is mainly all downhill and youngsters can be encouraged to take over the map reading.

Start: The free car park in West Street, Gargrave, which lies to the north of High Street. (GR932544)

Total distance: 14.5km (9 miles)

Height gain: 240m (790ft)

Difficulty: Moderate. Lane climb. Not to be attempted in the mist.

1 Leave the car park by the pedestrian exit, turn right and walk up Chew Lane towards the canal bridge, Higherland (number 170), which you can see from the corner of the car park. Do not cross the bridge, but turn right onto the towpath. Walk on to go across Eshton road to rejoin the towpath on the other side. Enjoy, as you go, the architecture of the bridges, the footpaths below the bridges and the working of the lochs. Then follow the towpath out in the gentle pastures of Yorkshire. Carry on for 1½ miles to pass Highgate swing bridge (173). After another mile you reach Thorlby Swing bridge (174), which you cross. Walk on ahead along a track, past a ruined barn, to come to the side of the A65.

2 Cross with great care and walk up the shady lane, opposite, to reach the hamlet of Thorlby. Go on past a small green and then up the steadily climbing way to reach the crossroads at Stirton. Turn left and go on ascending the narrower way and, after 1½ miles from the A-road, take the second footpath on the left, signposted 'Bridleway to Flasby'. This gated, waymarked

track leads out onto the rolling moorland of Skyrakes, with stunning views over Airedale. Look for the easy-to-miss signposted bridlepath, leading, right, from the track and continue on the wide grassy swathe that ascends through the rough moorland for 1¼ miles from the lane. Go through the gate onto open access land and carry on the distinct track through the rushy pasture. At a definite division of the track, take the left branch that climbs straight up to a stile, just before the heather-clad summit of Sharp Haw, 357m (1168ft), and its trig point.

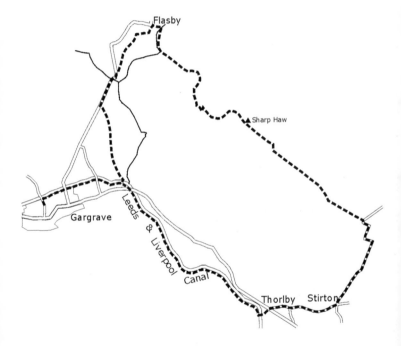

3 After enjoying the superb views, carry on along the continuing clear track and then, blessed relief for tired legs, the path descends to a wide grooved grassy track. Turn left and walk between bracken, which is soon replaced by a sea of heather (wonderful in August) to your left and Scots pine and birch woodland coming close to the track, on your right. Follow the wide path as it descends a little to come to a wooden barred

fence (hurdle), which you climb. Ahead two paths continue, parallel with each other. Take the slightly higher one, which is well trodden through the bracken; the lower one can be very muddy. Eventually the higher path turns down left for a few steps and joins the now much drier lower one.

4 Walk on through a long wide path with huge rhododendrons arching overhead. This is magic and all members of the family will delight in this 'tunnel'. Follow the arched way as it winds left and, as it starts to contour the hill slope the rhododendrons cease. Head on as the track turns right and winds on down to join a wide track. Bear right and walk for half a mile to reach a gate into a field. The clear track, now grassy, descends steadily, then winds half-left and brings you to a gate. Beyond, carry on to pass a cottage. Walk on through farm buildings, continuing ahead all the time, to come to a signpost where you follow the track left. Cross a bridge over the Flasby Beck.

5 A short distance along take the first left turn, with houses to your right. Just beyond, a signpost on your left, directs you right over a small stile and then up a paved way to a stile into a large field. Continue on up the next field, keeping beside the hedge on your left as asked. Climb the next stile and turn left. Walk along beside the fence to a stile hidden in the left corner. Walk on with fence to the left over a large area of parkland and follow the fence where it swings right to a gate into woodland. Walk up the little track, beyond, to a kissing-gate onto Eshton Road. Turn left.

6 Walk on, with care, to cross Eshton Bridge. Look right to see dramatic Eshton Hall. At the junction with the road from Malham, take the stile in the wall on your left. Go ahead across the large pasture, bearing slightly right to a stile. Cut across the corner to go over the next stile and walk on to join a farm track. Where this track swings right towards the farm, cross left to a stile in the corner. Descend the slope to climb the next stile. Beyond, cross the next field to take the stile near the left corner of the pasture. Once over, cross a plank bridge, climb the slope, slightly left, to join a path beside the canal.

7 Walk left to cross an aqueduct over Eshton Beck, hurrying on its way to join the River Aire. Walk on over a narrow wooden bridge and then after a few steps cross the footbridge above the end of the lock, just before Holme Bridge. Turn right to walk the pleasing towpath towards Gargrave and leave it at bridge 170 to turn left to complete the walk.

Along the Way

Britain's longest canal was constructed to provide a trans-Pennine waterway linking the emergent industrial towns in Yorkshire and Lancashire with the North American market via Liverpool. Work began at the same time from both ends, in Leeds and Liverpool, after the first Canal Act was passed in 1770. By 1816 the canal had been dug by men with strong muscles using just picks and shovels and working in mud in all types of weather. Reservoirs had been constructed to provide water to keep these vital commercial arteries open in times of drought. A winding route had been devised, following contours, to avoid as many hills as possible.

The idea of a canal to Liverpool first came about in Yorkshire around the 1700s. Many sheep were being raised successfully and a good woollen manufacturing industry had been established. But the woollen merchants wanted to improve on this by putting more sheep on the hills and pastures to obtain more wool. They realised that to do this they needed to improve their land and that a regular supply of lime was essential to fertilise the soil. They also needed more lime for mortar to be able to increase the height and size of their weaving sheds. A canal would transport lime from the Craven district. It would also allow them to send their goods to Liverpool and on to the emerging colonial markets in America and Africa.

Between 1786 and 1919 the Leeds and Liverpool made a profit; between 1820 and 1850 it made a huge profit. In 1972, the canal ceased operations after the last barge of coal was delivered to Wigan Power station. Today it is still in water along its entire length and is used by boaters and anglers. The towpath provides a grand highway for walkers and cyclists, with something different to see at every twist and turn.

Gargrave, with its picturesque cottages and teashops, lies on the edge of the Yorkshire National Park, between the Leeds and Liverpool canal and the River Aire. Generally the Aire, flowing alongside its main street (A65), dances and chuckles, but when in spate it rages, pushing the many ducks into quieter backwaters. After your walk you might find time to visit the village's fine 16th-century church of St Andrew.

QUESTA PUBLISHING

WALKS WITH CHILDREN

LAKE DISTRICT
Borrowdale
Buttermere and the Vale of Lorton
Around Coniston
Keswick and the Newlands Valley
Around Ambleside and Grasmere
Ullswater
Around Kendal
Around Windermere
South Lakeland

YORKSHIRE DALES
Wharfedale
Swaledale
Wensleydale
Malham and Airedale
Ribblesdale

PEAK DISTRICT
Dark Peak

also

SHORT WALKS
Eden Valley and the North Pennines

All QUESTA titles
are available from
PO BOX 520, BAMBER BRIDGE, PRESTON,
LANCASHIRE PR5 8LF
or by FAX to
0870 137 8888
Website: www.questapublishing.co.uk